URBAN CONTEMPORARY HISTORY MONTH

Poems

Margo

Hope you dig this!

12.18

SCOTT WOODS

Urban Contemporary History Month
Published by Brick Cave Books

All Rights Reserved
Copyright © 2015 by Scott Woods
Cover art © 2015 Scott Woods

Interior book design and layout by Integrative Ink

ISBN-10: 1938190300
ISBN-13: 978-1-938190-30-8

brickcavebooks.com
2015

CONTENTS

III. Muse Arcade

IV. Southside

I.
SOUTHSIDE

A REVERSE CHRONOLOGY OF SAGGING PANTS

6.
Hit the hip, but don't drag on the ground.
I only half mean I don't love myself.

If you can't find a bangin' belt, don't bother;
it's not going to work anyway.

Who needs to run anymore?
Nowhere we need to be.

Can't even fight no more,
hands clawed shut from jerking up pants all day.

Good thing I got this gun.
I'd never catch you with my pants like this.

5.
Adidas sweat suit
No shoelaces

Kangol to cardboard for head spins
You need the whole suit to match

You're going to lose your shoes
when you start breakin', so grab your crotch.

One day that's going to be the starting line,
my crotch. I know right now it just looks like

we're itching and hot.
Trust me: we have a plan to fix that.

4.
Berets cocked to the side,
standing in formation outside the precinct.

Goody picks saluting the flags of city hall
from within our afros.

Bell bottoms are like a cape for your ankles.
Where else you gonna' hide your nunchakus

and copies of *Soul on Ice*? In your dashiki?
A dashiki is a black smoking jacket

monogrammed with history.
Somewhere in there we changed names three times

in one decade. Kept the answer key in our pants
because dashikis had no pockets, not the real ones.

A dashiki with a pocket was a shirt sellout,
we used to say, not knowing that one day,

we would be able to type the word into a poem
and spell check wouldn't even blink.

3.
Zoot suits! Shoulders like battleship bows,
waist pulled up to your nipples.

If you ain't got no watch chain
she ain't got no time.

T-shirts are for catching sweat.
Harlem only pats you down when you leave.

Even the hoodlums got suit jackets.
Where else you keep a razor blade?

2.
Everybody on every corner wears a hat now;
the lawyer, the shoeshine boy, the cigarette hawker.

The diners are full of brim hats sitting patiently on stools
like dates thirsty for hot spit in overcharged Coke glasses.

A suit is a staple of civility.
Word 'round the church is we need civility.
You'd think it'd be a right by now.
The people who work in diners and drive buses

don't have to wear suits.
Perhaps civility is just how they jump you

into the gang of manners and shared
water fountains. We need at least that much

because anything is better than a Coke
full of spit and a smile when you trying
to feed your lady or your hat.

1.
Is it still a hand me down if you have to dig it out of the trash?
If it is already stitched with blood and coonhound reward?

If the pants have more briars than pockets?
Cotton rolled, thorn blasted sack cloth tunics

Shackles for cuffs, ragged sunsets for hems.
These are your work clothes, your church suit and your pajamas.

Ring it out every day off the side of your porch,
dry it with the sun or swinging from willow trees.

The thread count of a new/old pair of slave slacks is
immeasurable. You find rope for belt if you lucky.

Most days you think to use it to hang yourself, except then?
Your pants would sag.

If you run north, turn to page 9.
If you prefer a more fashionable nihilism, turn to page 12.

THESE AREN'T THE THUGS YOU'RE LOOKING FOR

Stormtroopers stop your hovercraft,
want to know where you're going,
what do you have in the trunk.

Broken lightsabres, you say,
desert laundry. Figrin D'an forgot
his gasan drum sticks at the cantina again.

Let's see some ID, they ask.
You wave your hand, steel your gaze, stating,
you don't need to see any ID.

They insist. You wave again.
They knock on your bubble window,
walk around your hovercraft.

You wave your hand again.
Didn't realize they were looking
for any of your kind they could find.

A gash of light, charred dissent,
the desert wind wiping away your chalk outline
like a Jedi mind trick.

If you keep your mouth closed, turn to page 21.
If you know your rights, turn to page 68.

PRAYER MEETING CHALK LINE

1.
Let's go see the NWA movie
like we weren't there the first time.

2.
Let's go see the NWA movie again
now that we know where all the jump scenes are
and don't have to miss anything, hiding our faces
behind our hands, waiting for the Dee Barnes scene
that will never come, hiding their hands
behind their faces.

3.
Let's go see the NWA movie and not wait
for the barbershop to get it first.
Wait in the line like regular folk.

4.
Let's go see the NWA movie while it's out.
Every dollar is a vote and every vote counts.
NWA was not rich enough on the first run.
Do you know how much a summer mansion costs?

5.
Let's go see the NWA movie
when church let out
settle into the seats
watch the screen
give praise all over again

6.
Let's go see the NWA movie
because the Public Enemy movie is sold out
the X Clan movie is sold out
the MC Lyte movie is being recast for a wider audience.

7.
Let's go see the NWA movie
and act like it's history,
like all the stories were not true
like all of the women are liars
like we weren't there.

8.
Let's go see the NWA movie
with our white friends so they can say
the n-word when they mean friend for one night,
and by n-word I mean "nigga I love you"
"nigga I see you"
"nigga I want to be like those niggas with you"
"nigga I want to say so bad I can taste it"
"nigga with flavor"
"nigga I adore"
"nigga hug me back/pound/fist bump"
"nigga I can take home to mom"
"nigga with the right attitude"
Let's go see the NWA movie
so I can say nigga with you and mean it.

9.
Let's go see the NWA movie instead of fight,
count the number of police cars in the lot
since the last time we saw a movie at this theater.
The last movie we saw had three explosions,
four shootouts, all of the bad words,
a gratuitous stripping of the heroine sans pole.
That movie was bananas. That movie was brimming
with death, like no one ever got shot in a theater.
No security that night.
So let's go see the NWA movie and get shot
by a real gang, by bangers who know the lyrics
as well as you do, whose colors don't run in the wash.
Who don't run. Who don't make them run.
Who don't run. Who gon' make you run.
Who don't run. Who swap chase for aim.
It will be so safe, with so many police waiting outside.

So many eyes on us.
So much attention on our every move.
I haven't even bought the ticket yet.
I feel safer already.

If you sneak into the theater, turn to page 5.
If you prefer our blues electric, turn to page 41.

WHAT I KNOW ABOUT CHICKEN THAT YOU DO NOT

If this is freedom I don't want it.

If I cannot tell you what I am eating
without the missionary tract
of a more responsible menu
that wants to starve me out of my utter blackness,
you can keep your freedom.

Shove it deep into your pocket,
where you keep all your rewards.
Poke it through your pants leg
until you tear a hole in it,
freedom running down your thigh like
grease and 'itis drool.

I am having chicken later.
That is what is going to happen.
It will be tossed in a Texas Mesquite dry rub.
It will crunch sweet under the teeth and tongue.
It is chicken even a white person would eat.
It is chicken a white person will cook
when I pay for it.

That is truth.

If you cannot see the me that has been standing here
because chicken is choking smoke and dancing suit,
then you keep that freedom, that freedom that knows
how I should talk about my dinners.

If I should have said "pizza"
because watching this mouth say "chicken" hurts -
        if that is freedom –
then show me that other water fountain again.
Make me wonder when you serve my food,
the slick of your throat buttering

my willfully ignorant steak and potatoes
like it used to.

You would have me lie about chicken
like I do not know it - its taste, its warmth,
its embrace of hot sauce and spices,
as if I do not pass your salted altars every day
as if you wouldn't dream of cholesterol as weapon
as if I should not lump you in
with white breast and dark lie.

And I don't.
I leave you to your yoga classes,
your right to review every black appetite
as if we have laid them out for you like biology frogs.
I should have said I was getting frogs legs instead,
tasted that affluenza inoculation shaped
like tender nuggets that smells like that good freedom,
that freedom that has no retort,
no smack of the lip,   no ancient stereotype.

Because that's how we know
when you're ready for freedom now:
whether you can keep chicken to yourself,
nibble at it quiet, under cover of freedom
that knows what's best.
That secret culinary criminality that makes
martyrs in the bloody driveways
and swamp-sunk station wagons
and Harlem ballrooms
and hotel balconies,
every chalk line easily avoided
by just ordering the salmon.

You don't know shit about chicken,
how it ran cold beside us in hobo cloth torn
from shirts, had to live in us for days;
how it bathes like an oasis in a desert
where you can't find a vegetable for miles.
How about I tell you which branding irons
still have fire, which blocks have the guns

that won't wait for New Year's Eve,
which of those old suits in the closet
that you remember us wearing still fit,
bones in their pockets from the moths
who have taken up residence, and,
as it turns out, also loves a good piece
of dry rub chicken and have been known
to speak surprisingly well for their kind.

If you go to Popeye's, turn page.
If you go to your momma's house instead, turn to page 75.

THE LIVINGSTON AVENUE SUITE

1.
The banner calls it the Livingston Corridor
like you could walk it. Like it has AC.
An Oasis water fountain
humming for you halfway down the hall.

Streets littered like trash tornados hit them.
The houses have as many clap boards as people.
They eventually replace the sidewalks
but never the buildings, like Jesus is holding
everyone's lease until He gets back.

Shoes on a wire make the clouds
behind them look like they're running.

So what, you want to sleep?
You picked the wrong baby's mama
to shack up with for that, son.
We don't have a lullaby that comes in
under a thousand watts.
Days end, even our slow jams are violent.
We don't sleep so much as give in from exhaustion.

Construction that never ends.
Guts of clay and steel. Naps of gravel.
A ghetto creek that ripples between orange cones
when the wind blows.
The cat tails we find in its shores
still stuck to the cats.

I was raised on the dentist that will let you pay Tuesday
for a root canal today.
Fero's Pizza & More;
it's the "& More" that keeps my eyes forward when I roll past.

The white person so crazy they get a pass.
A street trying so hard to be hard

no rap star could ever claim it.
There is a parking lot to nothing.
No business, no building, no sign.
Fence embraces with an open door policy.
Zones within twilight zones.

Businesses lock their dumpsters.
You don't see any homeless people on these stoops.
This a neighborhood, not no residential district.
Ain't no beggars on this strip.
If someone's asking you for money here
you're being robbed.

No check cashing place can grow here –
you either got the dough or you don't.
The tire shop
that was a martial arts school
that was a record store
that was a barbershop twice
that was a church
that was a tire shop again.
We been recycling for years,
before you gave it a color green was ours,
was money, was a reason, was a motive.

Miss C's Hair Salon & Tax Preparation:
because nobody out here makes enough
for it to be hard to tabulate their taxes
while having their hair straightened.

Queen Juqetta the First's reign
lasted 25 years before she was supplanted
to Whittier. Now it is Livingston Market.
The Gold Mine sells jewelry and teeth.

Club Tropicana's red lights, no front door,
windows covered in gates and cobwebs
red beer signs buried in a window
that will only ever be cleaned by a wrecking ball.

2.
The street signs are formality.
We navigate by barber pole and candlelight vigil
and where things used to be.

Sidewalks are largely unnecessary.
They wised up, stopped painting crosswalks.
We wore a path through the abandoned lot anyway,
a safari trail shorn smooth out of Nikes like machetes.
Three generations of revoked drivers licenses
have tripped over the same cement block.

She folds the same clothes one more time
in the last apartment left in the whole
complex with windows or souls.
Knows sections 1 through 7 like good neighbors.
They speak to her, tell her,
This not the way of things.
Liars. The walls are liars.
The floors, liars too.
Ain't a thing in this whole complex honest.
She's the last tenant in the building,
a ghost of clotheslines and flickering light
payments. She doesn't even get mail anymore.
She'd leave, but what for?
No one waiting for her anywhere.
And what greets her here every day
ain't got no name no more.
She folds the same clothes one more time
when they come to tear it all down
they will find a circle of hair rollers,
pink honeycombs laid out like Stonehenge,
a charred throw rug in the center.
They will wonder how it all got that way,
and the walls will answer in whispers
as they hammer into their sores,
blood quick roaches,
bones like bottle trees.

The Oakwood Sentinel
sits on his back porch half a block off the strip
watching a world too big for a camera.
He can change the channel with his spit.
I have seen him at every hour of the day,
like it was a job. They say he used to covet
the Office Lounge parking spots, but really,
he was there before they laid the bricks.

And so it's Saturday evening on the corner.
Must be date night!
Nah, baby, let's argue right here, in the street.
Let me fight for your love
where my efforts can be seen and honked at
by proper motherfuckers.
You make government cheese look good baby.
I got a band-aid engagement ring
where you cut me with your hair last night.
Yeah, that's the kind of love I'm talkin bout, baby,
love like styrofoam cups in fence
love like Walt Neil murals never touched by gang signs
kisses like garages you can rent
kisses like the Southeast Fish Market on payday
kisses like Buddha in a boombox
kisses like cranberry drank instead of juice
kisses like the clinic that looks like it prescribes illnesses
love like trash bag choir singing in the bushes
love like shrines with gas station rosebud memorials.
Fight me with your love baby, I may let you win.
Cause that's what Saturdays are all about:
fish platter feats, slow jams slippin out some 22s
and backseats til your momma out.
I'll take you wherever you wanna go.
I can make a living room a castle,
a dirt backyard a beach.
I got a way to bring everything in this world to you,
a hook-up on discounted realities.
That's my hustle baby: you.
God-givin gift of gab til you good to go.

Lemme tell you every barbershop secret there is.
Lemme show you love like
what makes music out of dust.
We got dust for days out here.
That mean we got music too.
Days of it.
Fight me with your love, baby
I don't need to win every battle.
Just the war.

3.
That the Linwood Red Door Plantation House
sits across the street from a hacienda,
which also has no business there
has caused more accidents than stray bullets here
is no secret.
Door blood-red like children have been
slain to keep The Angel away.
Upright, a mausoleum,
pillars like armless sentinels.
Who is it freeing?
Is its path more winding than a quilt can direct?
What plague are we averting with its swollen archway?
Which child was served like supper
for the rest of us to swallow?
What pharaoh's insolence are we suffering for?
The house says nothing.
The lights go on and off,
no rhythm. Another slave code,
another Angel of Death to scare away.

And the hoes!
Oh, the hoes!
The hoes you shall see!
Keep they money close to they heart.
Purses are for marks. That's what bras are for.
Muffin tops come easy, free.
Livingston hoes fill the whole pan,
make you want dessert where you have no mouth.
Pay for that pleasure with more than money.

Even the one in the wheelchair
knows a mark when she sees one.

Someone is building a ranch on Livingston Avenue.
Wagon wheel fences.
A tying post for a horse that will never come home.
Logs shoved deep where everyone else
would have put paneling.
It squats at the end of the street like a trading post
in the wild that isn't interested in sharing.
You have nothing with which to barter.
Or too, an outpost, a lonely last stand
against the last red men 'round these parts:
22nd Avenue Bloods fending off civilization,
casting their bottles into the front yard,
Thunderbird chased out so often
the grass won't grow.
It's not exactly the OK Corral, but then
it's not yet high noon either.

Now that Reeb Restaurant is gone,
there is a diner worth missing choir practice for in Heaven.
Today's special: the silence of progress.
Down here, there is a weed already taking orders
where your grandfather used to sit.
You still have to take your hat off
when you walk into Heaven's Reeb Restaurant.
It's not just the souls of people up there.
Love a place long enough,
it follows you home like a pet,
even through those gates.

4.
By the time you see Alum Creek Drive
looming in the distance you aren't sure
if it's a sweet sorrow or a finish line.
Where does the avenue end?
At the strip of bootleggers?
The crumbling train bridge spitting commuters out
like sunflower seed husks?
At the abandoned diner that doesn't know it's dead?

Or does it begin there,
at the stoop of the barbershop that sells
more DVDs than haircuts?
Is the smell of mackerel and ribs a trophy
for running the gauntlet or the smoke ring
from a starter pistol?

There are days when its
dilapidated storefronts slide into their dusk masks
sunset wiping its sweat
into their cheeks until they go gold like Tuscan hills,
their ancient awnings flapping dust like bed sheets into
the vineyard of toothless marquees.

I am not romanticizing you.
I am telling you that you are beautiful
because sometimes you are worth
the noise, the cyclones of gold teeth
the greetings like a wrestling match,
the small talk as loud as gunfire,
the kiss like a street fight.
Sometimes the rattle of trunks is a foghorn,
tells you
you are not alone in this ocean of
grime and tar.

I am not romanticizing you.
I am telling you that you are beautiful
because sometimes
you are.

If your go-to carry-out is Juquetta's, turn to page 33.
If your go-to carry-out is the 22nd Avenue Bloods spot, turn to page 23.

RULES FOR PLAYING "STAND YOUR GROUND"

Players must handle all weapons
with an extreme lack of caution.
Players may not negotiate.
Players may not share, only sell.
Players may stand their ground,
but only when armed.
Kings can only move one space in a backward direction.
Queens may move in any direction
so long as their kings are dead.
Players may pass "GO" only after
popping a New Year's round.
Players may collect $200 only after
finding where the bullet lands.
Players may survive.
Players may persist.
Players will lose.
Players should only be told this once armed.
Game ends when there is no one left to shoot.
Game never ends.

If #BlackLivesMatter, turn to page 21.
If #AllLivesMatter, turn to page 65.

DIOGENES LOOKING FOR AN HONEST COP

Diogenes looking for an honest cop
died with a burning lantern in his hand.
The flame consumed him kindling-quick,
his ashes lining the wine jar he called home.
They turned the jug up, fed grapes into it,
and pulped a most civil vintage.

Diogenes would have hated the cops
and the protesters, the K-9 units and the chants.
"Any march with a permit is the real crime,"
he would say, then scratch the master's dog
behind its ears, then spit, then look for matches.

Some say he was simply born too soon,
that his honest boon was dying for him
on a dark and dry hill. Three hundred years later,
he'd have found only the guards,
gambling on a dying man's loincloth
as he bled honesty all over the dice.

But then, Diogenes would have peed
on the hill alongside the dying, wondering
what all the fuss was about,
screaming "Don't flay me, bro,"
as he accidentally relieved himself
on a guard's sandal, a tear in his eye looking up
at the blooming rib of his dead king.

If you follow Him into paradise, turn to page 62.
If you prefer Texas Hold 'Em, turn to page 49.

(AR)REST ASSURED

if you open the paper
and read that i have been shot by the police,
rest assured

i did not run away
i did not walk toward
i know what arrested means
i was a good statue
i understand hands in the air
is more warning than ritual
i keep money in my front pocket
i am never reaching for a wallet
all my pants have belts

i was not hulking mass trying to take gun
i was not trying to take gun
i was not rushing, steeled for tackle
i was not magical or super-powered demon-face
i was under no illusion that bullets would fly off me
i promise: i was talking about downton abbey
and the sin of cold coffee
and hunting season bucks
anything to keep me alive

if they are laughing they are not shooting
if i am laughing i am disobedient
rest assured i was not laughing
seat belt tight like a noose
i was smiling in my license picture,
had insurance for my car, my time, my life
i had my music so low, my windows screwed tight
i was playing country music
promise: i was good boy
trust: i was not my race
i was not being my color/i was an invisible crayon
shoved in the wrong box

swear i was polite/not colorful
i was sans swag

i know what a bullet's job is
i followed directions, fell on first hit
i was as non-violent as i could squeeze into this body
i've been told if you're not violent you can survive this
lie still, lie dead before the bear
do not move when snakes rear up
my mouth moving over concrete cracks,
praying the whole time
to a god I am certain
used to kill things.

If you know your rights, turn to page 60.
If you're black, turn to page 62.

6 IN THE MORNING

My momma knew I wasn't shit when she called.
I ain't never tried to convince her otherwise.
Your grandma's dying. She askin' for you,
lazy motherfucker.
I said I'm busy, I be through.
She hung up.

My moms ain't never stopped puttin' a spare key
out back under that flower pot that kills everything.
Used to be she had hope for me.
She stopped hopin' when I went to county.
I know she just forgot the key was out there.
I get the key. I go in the back.
Smooth. Every day smooth, motherfucker.

Everybody sleep. This when I do my best work.
"Fresh Adidas squeak across the bathroom floor,"
swear to God, that's my shit. Nothin' in the world
make me feel like this 'cept dirt.
I ain't alive if I ain't fuckin' up your shit.
Some people graduate. Get jobs. Paint fences.
I steal cars. My career is the stick and move.
I paint sidewalks.

Grandma, she lie there. She not sleep.
She got an IV in her bigger than the one I had
when I got shot. Cancer's bullets is large, yo.

Grandma say, *"Come here."*
She the only one can tell me to do anything
and expect movement. My moms wanted to lace
the tombstones in her belly with baby shoes.
Grandma wouldn't let her, so Grandma get to tell me
where to go, when to come, and how the fuck long to stay.

I stood over her and she touched me
with a hand made out of old newspapers.

Grandma say she know what I do.
She hear things.
Neighbors talk to her when they won't talk to the police.
She say, *"I know you dusty from them streets.*
That you think if you stay away I won't know you.
That you tell yourself before every wrong thing you do
that we cut your baby pictures out of
photo albums so you can believe nobody cares about you.
I bet it makes pulling a trigger easy,
thinking you ain't got no family."

She tell me don't cry.
I don't know what she talkin' 'bout.
She kissed my knuckles like they wasn't rocks
like there was something in them soft, full of sunshine.

Grandma say, *"You an angel, baby.*
You got a trumpet for hands. I'ma need you
to blow that trumpet one time for me."
She tell me she cold all the time.
She don't eat no more,
that her nurses have lies for eyes.
She tells me she understands,
tells me in Heaven she can walk and sing
and swallow and shit when she means to.

Her pillow is the heaviest thing I ever held in my hands.
She smile at me the whole time.
She don't even move.

I put it all back like it was,
like she slept her life away.
I sneak back out.
Smooth. Every day smooth, motherfucker.
And I keep the key in my pocket
for when I come home.

PHYLUM

A group of poets is a salon
A group of assholes is a pinch
A group of rioters is a looting
A group of football fans is a celebration
A handful of chokeholds is a clutch
A group of terrorists is a cell
A group of suicide bombers is a war
A group of American terrorists is a militia
A group of black people is a gang
A group of black teachers is a gang
A group of black software engineers is a gang
A group of architects is a draft
A group of black architects is gang
A group of black American suicide bomber terrorists is a fantasy
A group of thugs is a syndicate
A group of black thugs is Sing Sing, is Rikers, is D block
A group of prisons is an industry
A group of groups is a people
A group of lovers is an orgy
A group of haters is a Monday
A group of gropers is a frat party
A group of assholes is a kegger
A group of keggers is a football riot
A group of black rioters is a riot riot
A group of riots is a movement
A group of movements is a society
A group of societies is a world
A group of worlds is space
A group of spaces is blackness

If you're partial to group dynamics, turn page.

TO THE MOTHER OF MY ENEMY

Here how he died: looking up at stars.
every constellation winking out
until only eternity left to mourn.
No angel came down for him.
His mouth did not part
with a choir's remembrance.
He did not call for you.
His peewee football uniform
ain't fit for years.
Sidewalk was a cooking stone,
even at midnight. Still, you could see
his last breath leaving.

You got nothing left to give:
another electric bill fell out your mouth
this morning while you were callin' around,
trying to find your boy, sitting
in a kitchen dark with roaches
blotting out the lights in an eclipse
of wings and mortar crumb.

Tell the media whatever you want
about your baby boy; the kind of work
he was looking for ain't the kind of work
you would have ever agreed to.

He didn't mention nothin' about no choir,
no honor rolls, no college.
If he had any dreams they mine now.
I pile them in my pockets until my pants sag.
Boys' dreams heavy with momma tears,
like pissed-on baby sheets.
Heavy, so heavy my belt just for show,
my pockets a vault of denim and steel
someone gonna' crack one day,
my dreams crammed in a dime bag
next to yours.

PRISONER #74234 SPEAKS ON YOUR COMMUTE

When you leave your house tomorrow
driving to that job you hate
remember not to dwell on the sun.

The sun is for your way home,
cubicle-spent, errand-weary, the spiders
of oversight tapping down your spine all day
sitting still in their kitchen corners for the night.

Notice only the gas needle, the dust
quilting the back of your steering column
like a slave signal (freedom is a loud and blinking left),
the grime tattooed to your cup holder,
the rattling trunk beside your own,
filled with liquor and pistols way too early.
Keep all of these things in mind.
What you work for is not in this place.

I do not go in the yard. I refuse the sun.
Recreation is mostly threat here.
Every ping of the ladle onto a puke-orange
lunch tray is the cracking of a home run swung hard
against a lover's sweating head caught buried
in another man's bliss. I used to jump at that sound.
A man shouldn't be scared of beans.
Gave away playgrounds and new music,
every tomorrow open to make a wrong thing right.
And most of me still believes that's possible
so long as there is no sun.

If you use the rock hammer, turn to page 37.
If ancestry dots the walls of your cell, turn to page 78.

KWANZAA AT THE SOUTHFIELD BUSY BEE SUPERMARKET

1)   Umoja (Unity)
They've spent three dollars in quarters
trying to divide and conquer,
one on the joystick, one on the jump.
Donkey Kong gets beat every level,
but that high score has been mocking them forever.
It will be three more dollars before
Keyon discovers that his gift
lies in handling the levels with fire,
Romie the levels in which ladders are unavoidable.
When they learn this, then they will alternate,
earn wisdom with every hammer,
salvation with every barrel.

2)   Kujichagulia (Self Determination)
I have come to expect more deference from others
when I am playing A Tribe Called Quest this loudly.
You don't know that they're not gangster rap.
All you hear is bass and the death of listening.
When they say we play the music in our cars
this loud because we're compensating for something
they're right; I am compensating for
shopping for expensive things under guard,
or arguing with grocery store butchers over
the weight of chicken.

This is not irrelevant to now.
You blew through that 4-way stop like I did not exist,
so I am following you now.
See me for what I am like you used to
and I promise you I'll keep on driving to work today.

3)   Ujima (Collective Work and Responsibility)
Two women barter

The last grease for the right weave
Fake nails shake on it

4)   Ujamaa (Collective Economics)
"I got five on it" tells you everything you need to know:

I = The leader, the One, the Id and the Ego,
the handler of all things. First to hit the weed,
the Shaker of The Bag, I, me, my.
The brains of the operation. Goldfinger.
He Who Makes Rain.

Got = Acquisition, get, got, took, shook,
shaken down, taken, Taken 2: Electric Boogaloo,
mines, lifted, annexed, no pain/no obtain,
procured, secured, stackin' chips, acquired.

5 = In the 'hood, everything is eventually divisible by 5:
34 ounces of Purple Haze weed cut by
6 parts oregano, multiplied by
3 dozen Black Man Handshakes,
2 baby's momma's samples
and 9 house parties gets you five.
Five what, remains to be seen.
Have faith in the formula.
Formulas are the American Way.

On = Toward, upon, here, now, in hand, certain,
present, right there, where we can see it, covered,
not a hook-up, real, the realest, kept most real,
palm grease on fire, done deal.

It = The eyed prize, the one ring, the treasure,
the curve of her thigh hitting right where it did
when you saw it in those jeans, pirate's gold, booty,
what was in Marsellus Wallace's case, the last supper,
Othello's pillow prayer, the light, to put out the light,
the rock, the essence, the sleepy song,
the largest bag ever smoked, the last drink, final call,
the over/under, the end of the night, the morning after,

the 8-ball in the corner pocket, the high, the beaming up,
the tingling that accompanies good customer service,
the thing, Gregor Samsa's applesauce confession,
high noon plus one, the Skittles, the sweet tea,
the answered prayer, the reason, the point of it all.

5) *Nia (Purpose)*
Every part of him believes
that he would pay for these things
if he could. Every week is only a matter of time
before someone sees his merits. If they'd just hire him,
it would make these trips unnecessary,
pockets heavy with cans, stomach bloated with air,
house decorated with need, heart's heavy hunger.

6) *Kuumba (Creativity)*
Tonight at five: Local brownie troop
gets creative with cookie sales
at a neighborhood grocery store
on the south side. Can you say
"make it rain?" More at five!

7) *Imani (Faith)*
She doesn't know how he knows, but he does.
You havin' a boy or a girl? he asks.
She is sure the test is buried deep enough in her purse.
Against her nerves, she says she hopes it's a girl.
He tells her from his daily perch at the cart corral,
his unnecessary summertime coat made of urine
and Thunderbird, that another name for faith is hope.
She looks him up and down. She has no faith, even now.
But hope? She has hope for days.

If you keep trying to break the high score, turn to page 69.
If it's a boy, turn to page 68.

II.
CLARKSDALE

ORIENTATION

Welcome!

…but sit in your assigned seat.

That stool belongs to Curtis Walker.
That one belongs to Ray Ray, even if he come late.
That one? That one belongs to Mama Confinia Nelly Jones.
No, not there either: that one belongs to the pharaoh.
That booth on the other side of them beads?
That belongs to the God of Pool Halls
and the table next to it belongs to the Swamp Folk.

This your seat, today.

If you lucky.

If you put sugar in your grits, turn to page 39.
If you prefer Junior Kimbrough, turn to page 91.

HOW TO BUILD A JUKE JOINT

Start with something that
wasn't never meant to be social:
a convenience store, a shotgun shack, a garage.
A garage is a fine start-up.

Wear it down.

Invite a friend over for a beer while you
workin' on their car,
every beer another point shaved off
what you may ask for someday.
put a radio in the back, behind the
toolbox, to make the time pass just-so.
Stop pissing in the corners and
take it out back.
Invite that friend back over.
tell him, bring his friends,
with change to spare.

Move the oil rags from the orange crates.
Move the orange crates to make room for folding chairs.
Move the car guts and steel jacks.
Move the oil bucket to make room for a cooler.
Move in an electrical wire spool and make table of it.

Run 2x4s and cover them in
whatever boards come to you.
Sheet metal will suffice, but
not above the Mason-Dixon line.

Remove the old light bulb and run
Christmas lights out its socket
until the ceiling disappears in
shadow or summer yuletide.

Set your rituals.
Don't bother with framing that first dollar;

you'll be spending it.
Make everyone tip their hats to the
Martin Luther King picture instead.

Never hire anybody;
everyone earns they keep the
old-fashioned way: ale equity.
A bartender who stands at it
when he's working and
sits at it when he's not
is ideal.

Know your regulars.
Advertise liquor you don't have to instill
hope.
Occasionally serve easy meats and
whispering pies.
Call drunkards by their traits and
only by their momma's names when
they can't come back no more.
Let the fast girls rub the slow men to sleep.
Let their pearls hit the dusty worn
cuffs of the farmer.
Let the deacon have the booth in the back.

Borrow the church piano and
never give it back.
Draw a line at the blues.
Let the nightclubs play music;
this a juke joint.
Give the band about three feet of space to work.
Make the guitar player sit in the audience
and the singer stand behind the bar.
They all want to anyway.
Call it Blue Monday even when it's Thursday,
but never call a Friday anything but payday.

Paint your dirty fingernails in class:
throw down a rug under the card table
you reserve for special guests.
Nail up curtains where there ain't no windows.

Have no dress code save the cutting eyes
of those who don't appreciate
things too new in the
vicinity of their shrines.
Keep it respectable.
(Respectable meaning, your sweatpants
can't have no holes in them.)

Put in a fan even if it will not
divorce the wet shirts from
their masters.

If the roof leaks, leave it.
You need the holes and cracks to let
the Swamp Folk come and go
as they please.
If Mother Nature sees fit to knock a
good-sized hole in said roof that
bypasses quaint,
every table then becomes negotiable.

Set up a lost & found in case
someone needs a hairpin or
the band needs a harp in B-flat or you
need a spare .25 bullet.
Keep your pens in a cigar box
and your cigars in your pocket.

Never put in anything new.
View decoration as either a
personal vendetta or a communal effort.

Make it the pimp's living room.
and the wino's heaven.
Let the tramps stamp it with their spit and
their knife-carved memories,
right into the bar.

Above all, own it. Never share it.
Brand it with your fists.
Tongue its tiles and pool stick-poked panels.

Swim in its flooded stalls.
Sleep in its booths and to the jukebox's
skipping 45s.

Keep makin' a job of it,
every night.
Never make it home.
That's everyone else's job.
Your job is to keep the drinks cold and
handy, and to make sure that
when the bulldozers come,
you don't have a tear left to shed.

THE GAME PLAN

We gon' fill that tub with all the ice we can get
We gon' tap them ACs 'til they can frost a screen door
We gon' set that piano up near the back
We gon' park that truck right in front

'Cause
somebody gonna' finally
        order that dusty bottle of sin and blues from the top shelf,
somebody gonna' heat this room up
        with they history and tears,
somebody gonna' hit a note that
        needs backing-away from,
somebody gonna' punch and run
        that needs slowin' down.

We gon' prop that screen door wide when the flies go to sleep
We gon' sprinkle chalk on that front stoop
We gon' run that juke box thirty minutes 'fore open
We gon' shuffle that dirt out by the back door

'Cause
somebody gonna' order
        them chitlins 'fore the catfish done,
somebody gonna' have the devil
        on they heels when they come in,
somebody gonna' need them blues
        soaked into the walls by the time they get here,
somebody gonna' be lookin' for they old lady's
        footprints from last night

We gon' spray that smell-good over the lid
We gon' shine our shoes and our pistols
We gon' forget names and faces
We gon' smile as much as we frown

'Cause
somebody gon' bring they lady tonight

that still believes in ladies,
somebody gon' need the fear of a
      whuppin put in 'em to keep the peace,
somebody gon' come lookin' for somebody
      we know and love with no love for 'em,
somebody gon' come tonight,
      ain't never been to no juke joint before.

SLOW DANCE SOUFFLÉ

1 pound of good game
1 cup of luck
1 medium car, finely cleaned
2 teaspoons instant smell-good
¼ teaspoon door holding
2 pinches choice of seat
2 quarts chicken wings, rubbed red hard
4 dollars in juke box quarters
2 ½ cups low lighting at room temperature
2 medium well house band, blues

Prepare stock over low heat.
Simmer car over medium speed.
Add chivalrous seasoning at juke joint door.
Stir until menu arrives.
Cover meal until eyes tender to the gaze.
Tip house band to medium low.
Serve over blue lights.

Serves 2 lovers.

If you drink the red wine, turn to page 43.
If you have whatever the bartender is having, turn to page 53.

THE GIG

You break a heart, sweat,
stomp a mud hole in them cats.
That's the gig.
It looks like we playin' music,
but that duck don't quack in this pond.
We journeymen,
afronauts divining the constellations hidden
in a cosmos of gin and sweet thighs,
pool chalk and swollen talk, big lies
and the lives to go with them.
We channel the gods you act like you
don't know. We pay the ferry
on your behalf every night.
Heard you cryin' before you
came in here. Yeah, we know that song.
We wrote that song, son.
Know that god by name.
You wouldn't know it if you heard it
but that's what we here for: communion.
To put in a good word for
you on the other side.
But we don't mind, son.
It's a gig.

If you're willing to play for beer, turn to page 74.
If you only play for money, turn to page 79.

THE GOSPEL ACCORDING TO BUDDY GUY

1.
"Buddy Guy."
That's almost all you have to say.

Self-made god of war;
cuts deep when he whispers,
cleaves past the bone and board to the floor
when he's trying.

Mountains lift their skirts and run
when that amplifier buzzes on.
Clouds check their tears in blue satisfaction.

His is the only guitar I ever heard
that I thought could stop
the righteous bullet of a jealous husband
in midair.

I imagine his strings don't break
so much as succumb to the will
of old cotton-picking fingers.

"Buddy Guy."
It's just about all you have to say.

2.
I was aware of the message
long before I heard the sermon,
knew the chapters if not the verses.

Locking eyes for one second
at a show in Columbus,
then another.
He double takes the young black folks
come to service.

In that moment,
that note was ours
and I became an apostle
of indigo stories in dusty tomes,
juke joints no child my age ever saw,
but have left sawdust in my shoes
just the same.

I don't know how one conjures in their mind
the notion to
pat Buddy Guy on the shoulder
as he passes wireless through an audience,
guitar calling down the walls,
leaving buxom salt pillars
in his wake,
but someone does.
Someone who thinks Buddy's
doing a "good job."

To me, this kind of homage is blasphemy.
Just because
Buddy's walking the room
don't mean he ain't runnin' things.
You don't bug God while he's creating.
That's how things like Starbucks
get made.

If you want to give praise
you don't try to shake hands
with lightning while it's cuttin' down trees.

You hush,
and you dance
and you wait for the sound of thunder
that's coming next.

If you spin Junior Wells next, turn to page 78.
If there is too much light for Junior Wells, turn to page 83.

THE REGULARS

1. The Good Shepherd

He blocks that 2 AM ol'-lady-call,
changes your paycheck for
jukebox feed and scratch-off wishes.

If you tip him
he will watch over you.
If you don't
he will merely keep pace.

Almost any amount of spare change
and he will wipe clean the crumbs of
silver dollar-card shavings that
used to be rent money.
He will spot you extra chicken wings and
levee-fed catfish,
have your tall-boy ready when
you stain the doorway with
your sorrow.

Any spare change will get you
a doctor whose every prescription comes in
shot glasses
a cigar-chewing loudmouth that hates you but
understands that every
working man needs to be able to
hate someone whose
hand be in they pocket;
needs to control some part of his
life, even if it is the warm and
final nickels out of his lap.

2. Pharaoh of Levee Lane

He rides in here rich
off the heartbreak of old men
who can't keep young love

3. Anniversary

He comes in
on the same day every year,
drops a fistful of
slow quarters into the jukebox's
begging slit –
every song a quarter,
five a dollar –
and we listen to
nothing but Etta James
until the cotton field-gold
sharecroppers and tail draggers
crash against the bar,
their tips and baseball caps
flotsam on dusk's shore.

He shakes his head on the
licks he loves like
clouds that make noise
when they pass,
fixes his mouth like a
railroad whistle when the
lyrics strikes his memory
with their moaning coal axes.

His investment full to yield
somewhere before the end of
genuine night
he sighs,
replaces a pork pie hat
straight and knuckle-cracking firm,
then shuffles off into the
smoke of barbecues in the

back alley,
his stooped back scanned long by
a cook's flashlight,
then the dark, then the
pickled and moist kiss of
pig tongues.

4. Monkeysong Jenkins

I'm the only child ever left on a juke joint porch step.
I got chicken grease for sweat and gumbo for blood.

I sleep to the sound of fading, drunk laughter
and end of the record scratches. I wake up to hung-over crickets.

Prison got three squares and a cot too,
but I don't have to play my own blues.

I mops 'cause it needs it,
but does it slow 'cause it likes it.

If you fall asleep at the bar they make me wake you up.
But I hear songs in it too, so I wake you gentle-like.

You can play any song on that jukebox
'cept F15. That's my song.

I met my mother in here once,
she didn't know it was me and I didn't tell her.

"Left my baby on the porch of a place
like this once," she said. "Better than what home I had to give."

I always sweep the top step twice as much
as the others.

5. Moonbounce

She dances with him and without him,
but never alone and never
to that song,
the one with the weeping guitar
the one that doesn't know she's
on her own again.

She rides moon beams that
slide in through old bullet holes in the ceiling,
curling the smoke from her dance
on their blue tongues.
Back bending, chest out to
gods and the serfs alike,
breathing in smokestack lightning
swamp gas horseshoe clinks.
Homeless but
with a bed everywhere she
goes.

She breaks things.
That's what they meant to do.
"Don't be mad when you
catch me wanderin' from time
to time, daddy," she warns them.
"See me fix on a slice of
early Sunday morning too bright for
church songs
catch my foot poppin' valleys into that
soft spot on the floor,
I'm just makin' my way.
Don't mind me."

She says this like tornado sirens
make destruction okay,
make it feel good while
watching your life spin away
into nature's Indian rope burn.

6. Top 10 Reasons Why This Joint is a Man's Best Friend

10. The one-stake horseshoe pit.
9. $3 admission for blues that cost
           $15 at the Blues Festival.
8. Catfish and Wonder Bread platters.
7. The bar is sturdy even if it is made
           from an old chicken coop.
6. The pretty women here aren't scared to get drunk.
5. You can sell the flyers for the shows
           to white college kids for $10 a pop.
4. Nobody knows if Muddy Waters
           really broke that window or not.
3. …but just in case he did, they ain't fixin' it.
2. Night fishin'.
1. Sign out front: Every Day Special.

7. Music Critic

His hands stop at a mid-G# blues
as the bass from the passing Cadillac
shakes the tale from his fingers.
"That," he mutters to the slaves nestled
under the front yard's sycamore,
"is no way to tell the story of your people."

8. The Frankenstein Lounge

It is the gatekeeper of lounges,
the Promethean lounge borne
from the graves of other lounges,
themselves shells whose owners have
left them by bayou banks,
ocean song whistling through chambers
lined with corn liquor silt and
moonshine varnish.

9. The Kiddie Table

The table shoved next to the end of the bar
is the kiddie table.
You sit there when you've been bad enough
to need talking to, but not so bad
your money's no good.
You sit there with your ear near
someone's ass until
they let you go.
You sit there, looking
at the wall until it
tells you its secrets,
detention bricks that knows
where the principal keeps his
fifth of scotch.

10. The Saint of the Playboy Club

When she went missing,
all her favorite records were
pulled out of the jukebox
and nailed to the walls.

We still lookin' for the boy
done told her that lie.

If you check the creek, turn to page 6.
If you know better, turn to page 9.

THE POOL ROOM LEVEE

1.
Some fool scuffed on in,
broke the dust line at the front.
That's how it started.

2.
There's one of her in every hall
worth its chalk:
Them hips too wide for normal chairs
Them ride too fine for normal fare
A tattoo right where it should and should not be
A cluster of smiles on each tooth,
one for every ship sunk smashed
against her weekly weave.

You keep a woman like that in your club,
you just beggin' for the Devil to come get her.

3.
He came in very un-dramatic;
no wind, no tumbleweeds.
Sideways, then cut straight.
The snake was not all out of him,
even with limbs to navigate.
Almost didn't see him in the tall grass of
moving bodies and
barbecue plates held high on their way
to scarred tables holding up
scarred people,
'cept he liked cherries in everything.

And he had a tail.

4.
The Devil pushed up on her,
all grins and scales in
a suit too red to be its true color.

And she smiled 'cause she liked red and
she smiled 'cause even brimstone
in the right amounts is sexy,
grabs all your senses,
shakes the shit out of you, and
she smiled 'cause heat is heat and
she smiled 'cause of Fridays and
she smiled 'cause that all she wants,
everywhere she goes: love.
Don't let that tattoo
right where it should and should not be
make a fool of you.

The Devil asked her if she wanted to go,
said he could stand her call and her rocky shores,
said he knew a planet filled with the kind of love
that could fill a woman with her kind of vacuums.

5.
That's when the juke box stopped.
We just thought somebody didn't like Ray Charles.
Had not yet recognized that the temple had been desecrated.

When the God of Pool Halls
came out of the only john in the joint
and looked about his garden, He was not pleased.
"Nobody works in here on Friday nights," He said.
"Not even you."

"I'm just here to dance, son," the Devil lied.
The God of Pool Halls was not pleased.
"This here my night off, baby," the Devil lied.
The God of Pool Halls was not pleased.
"Alright," the Devil asked, "What it gon' take to fix
that hat on yo' head right?"

The God of Pool Halls
ripped the microphone off the stage,
whipped its cord about His head
like a licorice lasso and snapped it straight
at the floor, a pool stick made.

50

Grabbed a beer bottle from a table,
ground the dust in His palm with a fist,
chalked that licorice stick bare-handed.

That Devil, he laughed,
knocked on the floor with
his shoe, heel to toe.
fixin' to race.

Wrapped onyx knuckles
on the side of the pool table.
Sunk the 8-ball without a stick.

That was the first game.

6.
It took Buddha, in all his jolly, infinite wisdom,
best out of twelve games to save a woman's soul once.
Took Osiris 24.
Odin? 29 games straight.
Jesus?
Jesus don't play pool,
but he has been known to lean
backwards over a table
for a popped-up trick shot once or twice.

The God of Pool Halls took 329 games to
do it right, most of them won on the break.
The dance was worth the effort, the
smiles He gave her genuine, the shrimp
fed her three bites large, the bend of her
legs more geometry than ego, the
exhalations offered all pushed back to
her for safekeeping. He even washed the
chalk dust from her body the morning
after with a slow sponge wrung of its
star sweat the night before.
It was all enough to change her favorite
color from Friday night red
to meadow green.

In fairness to the Devil,
and his howling all the way back to the road,
his strength lies in card games.

If you rack, turn to page 20.
If you chalk, turn to page 91.

THE SWAMP FOLK, THEY COME

The swamp folk, they come
        when the party runs late,
and all the shadows fill up with their bones.
The swamp folk, they come
when the band plays the old songs
        whose words only the ghosts know.
The swamp folk, they come
        when the party runs late.

If you're Cajun, turn to page 25.
If you're Creole, turn to page 69.
If you're black, press 1.

THROUGH THAT WAY

come in from Wanderers Creek
fill your plate with sweet meats and
the gizzards from ballads sung
in slave quarter voices of mythological proportions.

mind the beads when you walk in here.

the percussion of passage
a shower of bone chimes 'cross
your face,
red and gold car wash straps
dragging themselves across your
skin dry

drink until you have a half-filled
bar at your table,
'til your table looks like
the clean-up table.
make all future drinks from the drinks
you would not share
any other way save
you sipped their tips first.

stop in the middle,
halfway in, halfway out this world
stuck in ale space,
whiskey your co-pilot,
a trunk full of unsold bibles your cargo.

all things red in this world,
all cooing and the softest
ashy hands you ever seen
stroking the most beautiful
un-beautiful women you
ever seen.

the booth by the speaker

is the safest place in the world,
a womb with walls carved steep,
knife-tipped tempests from
purple lovers who brought
their nice blues into red places,
whispered at the top of
their lungs eulogy after eulogy
to the napes of pearl-lined necks
on saturday nights dressed
for sunday mornings.

CLARKSDALE

blackness scouring the source of darkness
blinded by courteous light in every corner
an international front has taken the beach
we are surrounded by good intentions

the juke joint host described as surly
in the visitor's guide is not pretending
people used to dance to this music
right after the moan
spread over a lie of land so flat you could
run your fingers across its washboard fields
and tune a thousand souls

stranger in a foreign homeland
all eyes on us, taking the measure
of the black folks without instruments,
come to see the blues zoo
please feed the animals
watching us watching them watching the blues
like everybody forgot how to listen and drink
at the same time
can feel the diary entry I am becoming:
saw a black man smiling at a blues show last night
knew he wasn't a local
tapped his toes in all the right spots

staying in a sharecropper cabin
refurbished for that genuine blues experience
even the spiders are imported
want to take every board and throw it in my trunk
build it over again where it belongs
burn it to the dark meat
likely the ground

somewhere in the world right now
there is a song playing
that will not end for a thousand years

it is not a blues song
it is a machine song
it is a system song
it is a caprice, an exercise, a trick
it is flight and fancy and ha ha ha
it is bowls and chimes and drones
all things you can play low and slow
into the grave
a song you meditate
that you travel many miles to hear
in very few places on earth
it will play for a thousand years
after all the black people have gone
and somehow for whatever reason
we will call that the blues

If you are a souvenir, turn to page 72.
If you opt for memory, turn to page 79.

III.
MUSE ARCADE

ANTISOCIALIST

Outside there is a bleating.
Not a normal bleating,
a possum or baby stray or coon.
Because I am tired and not supposed to be up at this hour,
I turn, waiting for what passes for nature here
to run its course.
This neighborhood is sick with strays
who have never had their claws
wrenched from them trolling about.
Survival of the fittest it isn't.
There are too many houses and trashcans fat
with what the beasts who awaken with coffee and duty
fill with our largesse.
We turn over when we hear things cry in the night
let nature police its beat.
There is never just one witness to a 'hood killing.
You can hear the mob like a noose pulling taut,
rustling through the dead grass of my backyard,
a savannah pride of haunts, a parliament of shushing teeth.
Without the bullets it's practically a lullaby.

I'm not the only one with an eye burning
in a 2 AM alarm clock sizzle.
The neighbor who holds court from behind
a new lawnmower every other summer
must hear what's happening.
When it all finally goes quiet, it turns out I cannot sleep.
Now a train whistle I have not heard in months blows
and I think, of course. How stereotypically maudlin
your death rattle has become.
It's so very human of you, to catch a ride that way,
o sloth of night, o eater of my garbage,
o render of trash bags and mulch piles
warm against your autumn belly.
You have got to be kidding me with the train horn.
That's some serious magic you're playing with there.
That's blues like a person plays

in the heat that only a killing
of city backyards yields.
When we see each other in the morning
on our way to our respective jobs,
we will nod or wave or salute coffee mugs.
We will have survived another night of playing sleepy god,
of feigned ignorance of how the machine world works,
of how even now, we still sacrifice to street gods,
of sweet rolling-overs when something called to us
in the night in need and we ignored it,
a somnambulist jury of its peers
because to hear the bleating is to remember
that there is no hunting season.

There is a hierarchy to feigning ignorance,
and we have learned from talented masters.
You know your place by how long
you cry into the night when your turn has come.
And when you die quiet,
with only teeth at your wake,
you can pretend you have finally arrived.

To weedwack... turn page.
...or not to weedwack, turn to page 79.

THE WHIPPING TEETH

Every few years we need new ones.
The old totems got a shelf life of one riot.

When you tell someone with a phone and a gun
in their pocket about boys like them
yanked by a mob from a train, you've lost.
Everybody thinks they're the one who would have
reached up and cut their own noose away,
spit back in a diner white with hate heat,
pulled out deodorant when the fire hoses
showered them with the hazing of scripture wrongs.
Old shows are for old ways.
Downloadable content, constant updates, memory refresh,
you need high definition oppression now.
Makes one long for the analog days of nightsticks.

We are losing our religions too quickly now.
We cannot keep up with our sacrifices
slipping into garbage can volcanoes.
You'd think we were Mayans, the way we let
our bodies fall in piles outside these projects
our hands reaching skyward, grasping at air,
ringing the streets like picket fences.
That's not fresh cut grass you're smelling.
That's not a sunset so much as a warning.

But then, the Mayans sacrificed prisoners of war,
kings they cornered and made bow down.
The old ways are probably still best,
as we are dethroned every day
and cannot keep up with the prophecies.

If you know a James Evans, turn to page 74.
If you were Huxtable, turn to page 77.
If both belong to you, turn to page 60.

MOST LIKELY TO RECEDE

Eighty-six percent of poets' bios mention
where the poet was born or raised.
Never mind that not one of their poems
was never written on that beach
or that island sound or that urban fire escape.

The wheelbarrow
is somehow informed
by the village:
the grease monkey
who only eats pie
for compensation,
the schoolmarm
defeated long ago
by resolution.
This is why
it must be red,
of course.
Red is the color
of sacrifice and
wheelbarrows are
the three-legged omens
of a heart you will lose.
And bay windows.
Lots of bay windows
facing no bays.

The word for it is perfect: juvenilia.
The footprints of poems passed before wiped smooth
across the sand to make way for what really matters.
I'm missing that.

My wheelbarrow
was my mother's,
and while it was red
it hauled gravel,
peat moss,

had no questions.
Kept no lists
on the backs
of prescription pads.

In truth, I kill
the children that fail me,
never inspecting
their cribs afterwards
for my handiwork.

If you use your funnynotfunny bio, turn to page 86.
If you don't feel like reinventing yourself in five years, turn to page 12.

TALK LIKE A PIRATE DAY ON D BLOCK

Warn any and all grandmothers too old for nightclubs.
Tell them their bibles are safe
but we have to change the books.

To wit:
Tell every out-of-work, Thunderbird-sweet uncle
at a cookout who's got it all figured out between
they wanderin' eyes
they prison-swoll tongues
tell them their dead dreams are their own now.
Gonna' have to walk that mile
with one set of footprints in the sand.

Reactivate the scholarship program.
The building fund is a wash.
Cancel the bake sales and the fish fry.

All references to the following:
"The Man"
"The White Man"
"Whitey"
"White Devil",
"Blue-Eyed White Devil"
"Cracker"
or "The Ghetto Cocaine Insertion"

…as pertains to the blaming of said personas
to any of the following:

a) your lot in life
b) your wardrobe
c) your breath
d) the media
e) the Boston you almost ran in a Spades game

…is heretofore devalued.

The word "nigger" is down three points.
Why isn't "thug" on the board yet?

It wasn't supposed to happen like this.
Not in this lifetime,
Not in this land.
They gon' let democracy die
before they put grape drink in the Oval carafe.
You'd think they never saw progress before.

Tyrone is positive he saw a virus-riddled pig
flying in coach yesterday.
When your president cries a thug tear
it's game over.

What's important now is to not point fingers.
No one saw this coming.
We thought that if we turned all of the old spirituals
into rap songs and dropped everything apple pie-hot
they wouldn't sing along.
We tried to make it nonsensical
and when they decoded it
we tried to make it abominable.
Our anthems so abysmally grotesque
they'd hide their babies while ours danced.
We got that one wrong. We underestimated
the entertainment value of our demise.
And to be perfectly honest,
we just didn't know anybody was listening.

If you go to the march, turn to page 98. Then get moving.
If you riot, turn to page 19. Then get started.

LURE

Little girl, nappy antennae
lighting out of your head,
tuning to see where that
loud music is coming from
don't be mad at your mother
for pulling on your arm
to stop staring at my car.
We play these things loud to feel alive.
We play these things loud to be rewarded
for surviving successfully another day.
I don't take it personal, and neither should you.
She's only teaching you how not to get taken
in by men that will not stay.

If you bumpin' Until the Quiet Comes, *turn to page 23.*
If you bumpin' You're Dead!, *turn to page 94.*

THE HONEYBOY THUG PARADOX

She falls all over his coffin,
her face a cursing river.
All out her mouth fall broken covenants.
She cannot hold onto her Sunday School lessons,
they spill out of her so fast.
She would give everything to be Abraham
in this Thursday night chapel,
sweating under God's will of chicken skin that knows
and casseroles stuffed with consolations,
all her cooking knives God-stopped in mid-faith air.

A teddy bear will disappear
from a chain-link fence tonight.
A dollar candle sweltering on a beer can
will waver, then snuff, then come back.
These are gods you can believe in.
They don't ask for much:
a gutter 40-ounce libation, the smell of gunpowder
at the end of a spades game, a pair of shoes
tripping over electric wires on their way to a forgetting Heaven.
These are consistent gods.
These are gods you can rely on.
Even the cruel ones who topple coffins under the weight
of mothers who cannot try again,
a banging prayer of wood and aluminum and amens
louder than a church organ,
promising, if only for a moment and slapping limbs
into her chest and cheeks,
her baby will dance again.

If you thought those were fireworks, turn to page 20.
If you knew they were gunshots, turn to page 27.

THE LIE

Security Question 1:
What was the name of your first pet?

     Petey.

Security Question 2:
What was the name of your third grade school teacher?

     Mrs. Clingo.

Security Question 3:
Who was your first girlfriend?

     A ghetto gypsy who favored chocolate cake & applesauce kisses
behind her grandmother's garage while playing "Married," in
which she was a school teacher and I a doctor who always had
time in the middle of the day to show up in her class and kiss her in
front of her students, who in my mind would go, "Oooo" and in
her mind were never there to begin with. She always left the
storytelling to me. Even at three she was very pragmatic.
Someone in that relationship had to pay the bills.

Type the text in the image below to prove you're human:

UNLATCHING

Papa Legba be the saint of pawn shops
and cell phone bars. When you speak to God
and he doesn't answer back you pray harder,
like he can't hear you.

When God don't speak you assume
he has better things to do.
I'll tell you from mowing both sides
of the fence: no god is that busy.

I sit here every day, waiting for your trinkets,
catch more prayers in what you get
for a wristwatch than God.
I hear you, but more importantly, I listen.

You want to know where your lanes go.
I can't tell you what Heaven's like. Never been.
Zombies Legba know well. All the best dressed
ones come from graveyards for obvious reasons.

Not what you wanted to hear, I know.
Legba not the answer. Legba a conduit.
When your prayer go quiet, then dead,
you already got your answer.

If God's trying to tell you something, turn to page 88.
If God's away on business, turn to page 91.

THE ODE NOT TAKEN

The road not taken my ass;
Frost had the road map on him the whole time.
I am not outside enough
to write great nature poems.
I especially despise the author pictures
where they have their glasses
pushed up on top of their heads,
like they were doing something important
and have been interrupted.
Don't you see that I'm creating, dammit?
I don't have time for really nice pictures
on the back of my first book in years!

If you go left, turn to page 49.
If you go right, turn to page 92.

A SERIES OF FORTUNATE LAMENTS

Let you have been white. Better,
Let you have been blonde
Let you have been hipster
Let you have been skinny jeans
Let you have been nerd
Let you have been dungeon master
Let you have been comic book collection in plastic
Let you have been mountain bike
Let you have been athlete
Let you have been quarterback
Let you have been owner
Let you have been old
Let you have been done
Let you have been tired
Let you have been leaning on everything as you pass
Let you have been remembering
Let you have been smiling as you recall
Let you have been youth
Let you have been rich
Let you have been dressed right
Let you not have been thirsty, let you have been sated
Let you have been choir boy
Let you have been better
Let you have been first in class
Let you have been best in show
Let you have been precious
Let you have been engaged
Let you have been on sidewalk
Let you have been obedient
Let you have been blonde
Let you have been unnamed
Let you have been left alone
Let you have been left alive

IV.
SOUTHSIDE

BLACK HOUSE PARTY, CIRCA 1979

Please be aware that none of it was ever a soundtrack.
Always a companion, or a prescription,
Sobek eating maidens off of the belly of the Nile,
a reckoning, a tonic, a promise.

We knew the four-beat was dying. We killed it,
scythed the mirror balls from every ceiling in every club.
Called the deed dead and done. Done baby,
done all the way down to the ground.
It was the grooviest mercy ever visited upon a crime scene.

Called ourselves Slave and Parliament –
the field uncovered in the exodus.
Called ourselves Tower of Power –
Babel rebuilding its vanity in every momma joke.
Named our heralds after mighty elements.
We weren't even trying to hide it anymore by the time
Prince rode in half-naked on a rented Pegasus.

You don't choose your gods
until your dancing days are behind you.
And for the record, no one ever actually
purchased a blue light for their basement either.
They just appeared in everyone's basement one day.
We used to dance so close back then
no one ever noticed Funk's purple-skinned engineers
going door to door – no knocking, no keys.
A mild invasion of privacy,
a knowing twist of glass in socket, and then?
Church was in service.

If you call her "Janet," turn to page 83.
If you're nasty, turn to page 97.

WHY MY MOTHER HATED TANG

Used to dream about orange juice then.
Tang chalk gritting my tongue before school,
that was the hard life. I could crack a Jericho floor

with a tantrum over a burnt Pop Tart
in five seconds flat. That floor wasn't even paid for.
Later, she slid a picture halfway into

an already stuffed family album like a new scripture –
a hidden scroll; Job the sequel, naturally –
never where you are going, never where you have been.

My mother, maybe seven, all legs and brown skin frown,
her mother a wall holding her sister's hand alone,
an upturned barrel behind them poses better.

The backdrop is a bleached patch of dead earth
behind a shack built too proud to pretty up.
Clothes sewn from white folks' husks.

A creek whose inlet was an outhouse, these people
could live fat on the space she made me weed every year.
I will never see her garden the same way again.

I swear that is a wagon wheel in the background,
and it is already old. It will buckle into dust someday, already has.
That girl that will already be my mother by the time we meet.

Little Mother doesn't know any more than I do,
but you can't tell from looking into that helmet
of mud and nappy hair like a drawn veil,

like she is being given away at a marriage
between Some Kinda' Way and What You Don't Know.
All of her pain is coming and gone at once.

And that explains everything:
every whuppin'   every second job   every sucked teeth dismissal
every hug that died on the vine of my ribs   every slammed door

every church slap for quiet   every birthday candle blown
soft and slow   every card that needed to be signed
"Love, Mom" for me to believe it.

And every glass of Tang shot rough down the throat
like all of the silt in the river where she bled
every orange in the grove gone sour,

nesting in my mouth, quiet, staring out,
every scripture whispered over a crib
cobbling a religion out of my ignorance.

If God is a parent, then He is my mother.
I have worshipped Her poorly. She would not approve
of the sentiment or the analogy.

I have always been bad at math.
Take the one away from me,
and in this book, we are still one.

If you don't even know what an allowance is, turn to page 28.
If you prefer orange juice, turn to page 53.

HOW TO MAKE NUNCHUKS

First, you need to know that
no one owned a car seat back then.
Pregnant women cut back by smoking weed
so a broomstick snapped in half to make
nunchuks didn't even register as dangerous.

The word *nunchaku* comes from the Japanese
Ryukyuan languages, loosely translated as
"latchkey ghetto child sleeping pill."

The chain could come from anything:
the worn teeth from an old bike, the bottom of a
now-dead grandfather's toolbox,
a kitchen junk drawer never explained.
Finding chain was never the issue.

Sticking chain to wood was the real
word problem, always starting with,
"Does your mom have any duct tape?"
ending with a smashed tooth on the ground
somehow your own, a feat you are
sure Bruce Lee never pulled off.
It is a *kata* worthy of a black belt you think,
even as the hiss of your mother's belt
comes quick out of the gate of her pant loops,
slicing the air with a matador's flourish
to the roar of children.

If you play as Bruce Lee, turn to page 81.
If you play as Jim Kelly, turn to page 26.

INDIAN IN OUR FAMILY

My grandmother was adamant about this,
attributing every decent curl on my head to
Indian in our family. Not an Indian; all of them.
Even at six, I knew this to be hyperbole.

"Indian in our family" explained her exquisite taste
in dime store jewelry, kyanite by the pound
at Sears, which was a boutique when you come
from Nelsonville and its miles of front yard flotsam,
jacked cars slumped before every house like stone lions.

My taciturn grandfather had it too, Indian blood.
It did nothing for his hair, and I was not convinced
that the stoicism he wore so well wasn't due
to the white people he shared a coal mine with,
their tongues blacker than his skin.

At six I was sure that our Indian had to be different,
a hunter with no patience for traps,
all his kills by arrow or sarcasm. Once talked a buffalo
into shuffling off its pelt after a debilitating round of dozens,
greeted everyone by saying "Why" instead of "How."
Our Indian, he would have kept Manhattan Island,
but never cut the grass. Called it "keeping it real."

For years I watched my brothers beached
on couches after holiday dinners, the plankton of greens
and yams swimming into their mouths like a calling.
I wonder which people we got swimming from,
if our Indian had good appetite to go with good hair,
which I see now, crumpled against a couch arm,
cheering for the Redskins to go all the way this year.

URBAN LEGENDS

If you flash your headlights at a dark car in passing,
it is a gang initiation and they will kill you.

Gangsta rap crawls into your ears while you sleep
and puts black people in your dreams.

The 13th floor of every office building can only be cleaned
by a black janitor with very good luck.

A chicken head once found a deep fried politician
in a bag of crack.

The sewers of New York City are teeming with extras
from The Warriors who got lost on their way to the set.

If you do not pass this poem on to five friends,
you will still have read more than any three congressmen.

Swimming in less than an hour after you eat cheese grits
will cause you to sink to the bottom and drown, but with a smile.

Over a dozen black morning radio show cruise ships
have gone missing in the Bermuda Triangle.

If you lock a hundred monkeys in a room with typewriters,
a hundred monkeys will type Lil Wayne lyrics.

If you stand in front of a mirror and chant the word
"Obama" three times, Ben Carson will appear.

If you are Scully, turn to page 86.
If you believe, turn to page 65.

HAVING DINNER WITH SARA LITTLECROW-RUSSELL

I am having Chinese, but not real Chinese.
She is having French toast, not frybread.
We are so intercontinental right now.

"Tell me again how hard tough ghetto is."
I wouldn't know, and she knows this.
All of our trivia is who got shot first.

You have to admit, I say, *that cotton gin was something.*
"Show me the way to a buffalo and I'll show you
How to fish for a career in sanitation management

For the rest of your life." It is my turn to be drunk,
to say too much and blame the dust in my throat.
It is a rain dance made of momma jokes:

There are too many of us left to give out casinos.
All of our poker chips would be barbecue.
At least you were on a nickel for a while.

It all sounds better in my head, where the cornrows
I am compelled to mention have been harvested
by coyotes that speak better English than I do.

If you tell her the one about the barista,
the DJ, and the librarian, turn to page 99.
If you eat in silence, turn to page 37.

DENNY'S DINER AND COLOSSEUM

A Denny's fight video always starts with an eruption.
The tremors are all of the neck rolls in the world,
then there is a face, moving, too close to her,
the snap of a head at the end of an acrylic fingertip,
and then it's moving day.

Salt shaker missiles fired from the silos in their chests
from a post-club high, the booty call not yet answered,
the jam that made dancing in them heels with that t-shirt okay.
The Grand Slam breakfast is three scrambled eggs,
bacon or sausage and a side of your weave pulled out.

With a flash of thong, a glimpse of a mole
nobody sees but her man, this should be sexy, but it's not.
Everyone becomes a filmmaker, phones taking it all in,
unblinking Cyclops of infamy and electric eternity.

When I saw my mother wield a skillet
aimed at my brother's head, I shook for two days.
My meager belt-to-ass violence paled next to it.
Now, seeing a Santa Fe Skillet fly through the air,
eggs in her eyes, hash browns in her locks,

I am amused, even when it finds the soft place
in a woman's jaw to land.
There is no family to consider here.
None of these women – always women –
belong to my gulag.

The kids at my job watch street fights all of the time
like it's a job, a generation raised on thugs that can't fight
or keep their pants up to run from their mistakes.
A mirror in front of a mirror
eating itself until it goes black in the corners.

They don't know what real violence looks like.
It looks like a face with maple syrup for tears,

trying to defend its honor by pulling down a skirt
too short for brawling or this time of year,
as if that was what we were looking for.

If you order the Grand Slam, go to next page.
If you don't get served because you're black, go buy a book of
Etheridge Knight poems instead.

MY EX BY WAY OF REVIEW

If you don't have a reservation, expect a wait.
Call well in advance. A reservation can be hard to get
and it is not uncommon to arrive and find
someone sitting at your table, eating your lunch.

If you discover you're part of a large group
reserve the communal table in the back,
which seats up to seven large gentlemen at a time.
Follow the locals to one of the best openings in town.

Dress accordingly. If you find that you haven't, fear not:
she will pick out all of your clothes for you anyway.
For the price, it's almost totally not worth it.
It is an outrageous value for a relationship of this quality.

You'll be thinking about this one long after it's gone,
a hint of cold spaghetti on the tongue,
a whiff of Spanish lotion in an old letter,
with a finish ending in a three month tryst with her old boyfriend.

Consider visiting in the spring or summer,
when her dresses are as short as her temper,
but reserve in advance: popularity and size limit the availability here.
Order the heart, rare. If it's not on the menu, ask for it anyway.

TO THE UNCUT LAWNS OF SUMMER

First Cut of the Year
    At ten, he already knows what I want to hear.
    At ten dollars it's practically a steal.
    Having hooked my laziness by the lip, he asks –
    ever the professional - if he can use my lawnmower.

    By the end, my yard is so full of patches
    I expect Brer Rabbit to come bounding out
    from behind the knee-length pentagrams
    my hero has left behind.

    If he were my child I would flay him
    with a weedwacker, except it's another
    ten dollars to let him borrow
    my weedwacker for the privilege.

Watkins Elementary School
    Sitting in a third grade classroom,
    I would scan the field behind the school

    to figure out the best place to kiss you
    where no one could see.

    They've put more school there now,
    plopped a cafeteria where our hiding weeds used to be.

    I hear they serve our love for lunch these days,
    my wandering fingers warming hot pack pizzas,

    your lips pressing out from under the plastic tops
    of every fruit cocktail cup.

Eddie's Bike & Mower Service
"Barber always need a haircut," he says,
    spitting a period into the band-aid of lawn
    beside his store, their fingers reaching
    our knees, my hip, my wallet.

That Neighbor
 The sun x-rayed the icicles left hanging off the gutters,
 a patch of green melting into view beside the mailbox.
 "Tina! Bring me the scissors!" he said without looking,
 damned if anyone was going to cut their grass before him.

Watch Your Step
 (don't be fooled by my wagging tail;
 i want to be difficult.
 watch you hopscotch across this lawn,
 worried and picking over my gifts.
 there has always been a symmetry
 to this you have never noticed.
 if you had left my piles where I placed them
 you'd know about the aliens
 who move your keys at night
 and stand over you as you sleep,
 stealing your refrigerator magnets one by one,
 wondering why you keep your food on the outside.
 i tried to warn you.
 true to form, you do not listen.
 they are not anal probing you.
 they are trying to give you tails.)

Field
Every day, cerulean. Every dream, stillness. No teeming fingertips like
tongues. Windless time, air that knows how to be quiet. Pollen in my
hair. Somewhere a lawnmower is chewing at my lovers. The first thing I
remember was not seed but sun, each of them breaking my skin to kiss it
before I knew what a covenant was. No word, no reason. The sun boiling
my veins for dinner. Bring me winter again, for real this time. Wage your
snowball wars across my legs. I like that. No one knows tickling like
a child. Lovers come close, their blankets thrown careful, then mussed
almost immediately. I am not a floor, but given enough time, a hush of wind
cooling their anticipation, you might get it right one day.

If you wait until the weekend to cut, turn to page 37.
If you try to beat the rain, turn to page 63.

THE JANITOR OF *HIGH SCHOOL MUSICAL* SPEAKS

Do you have any idea how hard it is to get
sneaker prints off of linoleum that's been carrying
an entire high school's weight
in singing, dancing, raging hormones?

I mean, I just waxed that floor.
They got a gym that's never seen a basketball.
What's the point of a gym when every hallway,
desktop and bathroom stall is an invitation to The Dance?

Every pine-scented bucket I have is filled
with dingy water and the sweat of their dreams,
which I could more easily admire if I weren't cleaning
up after them every other period.

Every time there's a fire drill they file out of their classes,
twirling, arms in the air, single file all the way to the curb,
where they jump on the nearest car, bopping their necks
to the rhythm of a fire alarm.

They moonwalk in midtown intersections,
halting traffic, jumping up and down on people's cars,
then drag they funky feet into the cafeteria
like they've been dancing on air.

I just washed those tables, just emptied that trashcan
Troy is spinning over his head like a damsel in ballet distress.
Like they don't have trash cans at home.
Like their parents don't mind that they practice
their jazz hands while passing the mashed potatoes.

Their idea of intramural sports: choir practice.
Varsity Sculpture. Full contact macramé.
No books, no library, no showers.
By 2:30 I'm ready to nail some ballet shoes to the floor.

None of them realize that they're just one bad knee
or failed recital away from having their name
on their shirt for a living, rinsing out some
self-absorbed kids' dreams in a mop bucket.

If you dance, turn to page 9.
If Drama Club is more your thing, turn to page 6.

NEIL DEGRASSE TYSONS'S LOVE NOTE, THIRD GRADE

Dear Shaniqua,

In 1932, when F. R. Moulton said:
"There is no hope for the fanciful idea of reaching the moon,
because of the insurmountable barriers to escaping the Earth's gravity,"
he could not have conceived
that I would see you across a playground,
hanging upside down by my knees
from a set of monkey bars,
and that, upon noticing all of the beads
clicking against each other
out of the nautilus of your braids –
10 percent of the blood from the bottom 50 percent of my body
leaning into gravity at a rate of approximately 5 liters per minute –
that my heart would breach this resistance
and forever search the heavens for love.

In 1901, Wilbur Wright once turned
to his brother Orville and said,
"Man will not fly for 50 years."
The Wrights did not then possess the inspiration
to fathom that one day this letter,
folded into a paper airplane,
would fly to you through springtime classroom air
at an initial launch rate of 50 miles per hour
with an optimal 10 degree vertical
and a front weight of 2 grams,
not counting the cargo that is my love.

My heart is a centrifuge.
I am sure a poet has said that before –
I have too much math homework now to uncover whom –
but rest assured, they do not know what I know.

A centrifuge puts an object in rotation around a fixed axis,
applying a force perpendicular to its axis.
Using the sedimentation principle,

where the centripetal acceleration causes denser substances
to separate out along the radial direction (the bottom of the container),
with lighter objects moving away and to the top of the container.

In short,
the relative centrifugal force is equal to
the rotation radius times the angular velocity squared,
divided by the earth's gravitational acceleration.

We use it to separate isotopes.
We use it to separate sugar crystals from mother liquor.
We use it to separate solids from drilling fuels.
We use it to separate cream from milk.
We use it to separate the rinse water from our clothes.
We use it to separate tolerance from the cracks in astronauts.
We use it to separate man from earth.

Ergo, my love,
my heart puts your smile in rotation around my soul,
applying love perpendicular to my being.
Using the tendency for feelings to settle out of my racing blood,
where the daily anticipation of you stepping onto our bus every morning
causes my dense fears to separate out along the pit of my stomach,
with intelligent conversation and common sense moving away and
sticking to the top of my skull.

In short, my love,
the relative centrifugal force is equal to
GOD I WISH YOU SAT CLOSER TO ME IN CLASS.

We use it to separate our innocence.
We use it to separate the boys from the men.
We use it to separate living from mere life.
We use it to separate promise from extinction.
We use it to separate longing from waiting.
We use it to separate dreams from the cracks in naptimes.
We use it to separate man from earth.

I take it back: no poet has said it better.
No metaphor is stronger than the physics it masks.
All of which is to say, will you go with me?

Will you enter into this play fort I have made from boxes and coats,
this ship of the imagination,
carry this spinning heart with you
beyond the horizon of all telescopes,
dance like Andromeda kissing the Milky Way,
until the stars wink out one by one,
or until your bus arrives,
whichever comes first?

If you're still arguing that Pluto is a planet, turn to page 79.
If you knew Gravity *was ridiculous, turn to page 60.*

BOOMBOX OF THE SPHERES

The music of the actual spheres is Wagner
and Beethoven and Salieri.
It is ballet and brass and vast caverns of ambience,
spilling beauty and dismemberment in equal measure.
And, depending on the equinox, a couple of timpanis.

The music of black holes is new age,
Tangerine Dream dragging everything it touches
into its gaping maw, putting it to sleep forever.

The comet tail is reggae, slipping past quick,
an illicit and dangerous orbit if we are lucky,
the sizzle and flare of smoke and fire,
under darkened porch, under red light gone slow.

By all accounts, the Big Bang was the first rap song,
all bass, a tidal vibration of everything happening at once,
every trunk rattling the bones of Carl Sagan and God
is a lonely person screaming back at the universe,
demanding to be heard by any and everything,
wanting to remake the world in their image.

This is why people fear it,
why we turn our heads at red lights
like we can't see new planets coming;
why police must be called to reign in its dull destruction:
some people want things to stay
exactly the way they are.

If you bump "Lollipop," go to page 6.
If you bump "How Much a Dollar Cost," go to page 96.

THE REQUISITE NUMBERED STANZA POEM

1.
This is where the poem begins.
Or starts, ergo, 1.

2.
I was supposed to transition here using resonance,
or failing that, I was supposed to use my words.
I didn't. I used my numbers.
Well, I used one number.
Not 1. It was 2. I used two numbers here.

3.
Somewhere past the valley of our final disagreement,
you asked me for a poem.
To compose it for you.
I want to make you think this is that poem
and it's just being extremely subtle.
As it turns out, it's about something else,
about math and insecurity,
about how I have used more numbers than devices here.

4.
I should have broken those last two lines up with a number.
They kind of diverged there, and every time I came up with
a run of new thought, I was going to put a number on it.
I'll do it now:

5.
About math and insecurity,
about how I have used more numbers than words
we have shared face to face.
Every time you see me you run. Then you blow my phone up,
wondering why I didn't suggest more numbers.
By numbers, I mean more thoughts.
I use numbers to show you how many thoughts this poem has.

6.

I take it back: this IS the poem you asked me for.
I just didn't know it back when I said 1.

7.

I loved you when you loved me back, hand to chest,
cleaving desperation out of your stomach like new testimonies.
The valleys aren't as low as we thought they were.
It is that the hills are rising. You are sinking.
It looks like swimming, but I can tell
by the way you take in water
that you're not yet as buoyant as you thought you'd be.

8.

This is not a list poem.
A list poem doesn't use numbers this often.
List poems just go from one grocery item to the next,
a loaf of bread, a gallon of milk, your heart,
my back of scratches. No math, no emotional parabolas
juxtaposing what you can stand when.

9.

I had an idea for a poem, but it didn't come from me.
I was what you'd call inspired.
I didn't write that poem.
I wrote this poem, this poem about you,
and numbers, and how all of the times you asked me
for something that wasn't a piece of me you could see
fit cleanly on this list.

10.

Except this isn't a list poem.
This is a poem whose stanzas are numbered because
I did not trust you to follow me into this place,
and I did not know how else to convince you to stay.

If W. D. Snodgrass, turn to page 101.
If Phonte, turn to page 74.

SIDEKICKS

The old professor who crooks the wisdom knot at the back of his
head on the cool metal of a coffee shop windowsill
and remembers an old Tuscany in May

the lonely street preacher throwing salami sandwiches
into the maw of his belly at lions with
patched manes and steel tails

the two kids skipping school
to play the last Pac-Man console in the
last greasy pizzeria in town
with lunch money
high score dreams

the sister-girl prayer group and Thursday night closet book club

the Livingston Avenue jump-rope championship squad

the boys playing pirates in treasure-less dust
the three-legged dog that hates water
the prostitute's last leg-up
the lippy boy in the mall
the old
the park bench warmers
the pigeon feeders
that one girl.

These are not our victims,
spin tragedies on their fingertips quick.

When the guy in the red cape
smashes the ten-foot alien through an office building
with a nearby Cadillac
it is almost never like you see in comic books;

broken glass
and flying bricks
and four-colored astonishment and awe.

Nothing vaporizes.
Everything finds a place to land,
to be.

When you live in a world where people in their
pajamas break things daily to broke tragedy,
the irony is never lost on those of us left behind
who don't wear masks to work.

You either walk around loving everyone
or no one
because the glass must rest its wings,
the bricks must pocket themselves somewhere warm.

The school teacher who happens to die in battle,
screaming from behind the wheel of a used Nissan Fox
as all her car payments end in the
name of truth and justice,
the papers will call her a victim.

We stopped trying to convince them otherwise
years ago. Those of us
who walk in the shadow of human landmines
and blonde bombshells that actually explode
and capes that drape thick necks like flags,
those of us who make our way in
slow, people time,
we do not call them victims.
We call them sidekicks.

If you buy DC, turn to page 88.
If you're a Marvel head, excelsior!

JESUS WEPT, THEN SULKED A LOT

It is easier for a camel to go through the eye of a needle
than for a poor man to enter your apartment on a Saturday night.

Behold, I stand at the door and knock.
If anyone hears my voice and opens the door,
I will come in to him and eat with him.
If anyone doesn't open the door, I will assume the worst,
and stand in your front yard with a boom box,
playing "Drunk in Love" in a trench coat
and wail mightily until you roll from on top of that guy
you met at SXSW with the soul patch to match the suture
he has stitched onto your soul where my love used to reside.

Follow me and I will make you fishers of men.
Follow you and you shall make me restraining order.

Let the one among you who is without sin
be the first to cast a stone,
as I already have two strikes in this state.

As the Father has loved me, so have I loved you
and each of your pillowcases. And your panty drawer.
And that one picture of your mother in Cazumel in 1987.

Happy are those who are hungry and thirsty for goodness,
for they will be fully satisfied, save that they date you,
and shall never fill the howling black chasm
of your malevolent and depleted soul,
which makes the curses of Revelations
look like a Reading Rainbow marathon.

And know that I am with you always, girl; yes, to the end of time.

If you put Kirk Franklin on your mixtape, turn to page 40.
If you opt to use Commissioned instead, turn to page 70.

THE ASKING

praise. poems written on the feet. as deep inside as possible. hands. a
new language made of hands. warning strokes. kiss of one thousand cuts.
replant all the dead lilies/water/wait. bloom the breast. blush the cheek from
afar. turn gold to night. kiss the scars. scratch the scalp. be wind across
cornrows. know it. side eye sigh. be lascivious. be wrong to it/apologize
with your fingernails. sing into it. expose it to moon. expose it to the rain.
expose it to the moon in a backseat rainstorm. make it storm. make a beach
of its bed. bury it in the sand. call it sphinx and ask it questions. do not wait
for the answers. hold it up. have it hold it up. wait for it. split its folds. kiss
it folds. lick its teeth. make a kiss feel like a punch. map its constellations.
tattoo it with tongue. work its limbs. send it flailing across the planet of
pillows you have discovered in search of air. punctuate. trace its ley lines.
build a place of power in its belly. bite the back of its arms. fill all holes.
make new holes. fill all holes with unexpected things. stay pleasant. do not
stop that until the mouth cracks open. do not start that until it says your
name with its palms. make it smile where it has no lips. tan it where no
light can see. crown its feet. name its parts.

the whisper. the marker. the bend. the spread. the massage. the pump. the
razor. the savor. the suck. the mouthing of words. the bruising. the past.
the comb. the blowing. the time. the back kiss. the freeing. the dismay. the
moaning. the unfolding. the devil-may-care. the drive. the shuddering. the
toss. the play. the curiosity. the scholarship. the flex. the help. the patience.
the strength. the tasting. the quickness. the length. the science. the will. the
engineering. the gravity. the repurposing. the sense. the religion. the hunger.
the presence. the piercing. the angles. the character. the resilience. the
stigmata. the curving. the rubbing. the adornment. the permission.

ADAM'S RIBS & CHICKEN & BISCUITS

I have loved barbecue like I have loved you
stoked in the mesquite fire of a black bellied stove, flamed with attention,
fought with drunken men over the best parts, swallowed hard.
Set to watering a mouth full of summer gunshot
slathered it with secrets and longing.
Whispered cursing prayers into the heat to make it last
just one minute longer in the wavering fade of August.
And now you are thinking, *he just compared me to a meal*,
which is not what I have done at all.
I have compared my gods to you,
given you back that stolen rib and made a meal of it.
Look at me. This is no trifling game.
I worship at my altars daily and my Gods
have tried to kill me twice this year,
once by driving my blood into frenzy, salting my veins,
doctors everywhere bowing their heads.
And then another time while I was driving,
my car filled with the hymn that only a bag of pulled pork knows the lyrics to,
plastic clinging to the sweat of its styrofoam,
jarred by the acrid burn of tire screech as I peel myself out of a seatbelt,
engine gone, windows eggshelled all over me
while I lick the evidence of my complicity from my fingers,
smacking lips of love and sauce in my palms
It is a crime usually reserved for driving while writing poems,
but then I am an acolyte of many pantheons, holy ghosting out of me
all of the ways to love you.

If you like your chicken fried, turn to page 9.
If you're a vegetarian, turn to page 68.

INFERNO

Everybody compares you to angels.
I don't want any fucking angel.
I want you to love me like
I'm going somewhere hot for the crime.
Love me like there's no tomorrow.
I am in my Sunday suit already
tugging at the coffin rings, pulling the lid down for privacy.
Show me how they lick their lips in the ninth ring
Let us set Dante's ass on fire.
I want you to write poetry on my skin with a ballpeen hammer.
Show me how they get it done down there
where there's no water and the sweat evaporates
as soon as I make your skin speak it's language.

They're gonna' call what we do impure.
Tell us we're a fraud.
Fuck 'em. I want nine cock rings – large –
One for each grave sin we will commit
and each dark place we will stuff in one another.
A gluttonous love, a passion so full of your mouth
you can eat yourself. The cousin you hate
is dropping her baby on the kitchen floor right now
as I kiss you, all teeth, forked tongue.
If we are good, she will break a hip in our honor.

When we are done, I want to gaze at the moon
look at its craters and holes and wonder
if I can plug every hole with myself.
I want to fuck Stephen Hawking's ghost
for even making me think that.
But who cares? Throw that crime upon the pile of shit
we will share in a cup anyway.
Ring up the curator at the museum of purgatory!
Tell him the Hannibal of sex and farm animals is coming!
Roll out the carpet of tongues
so that we might rut around on it as we approach;
have your concubines already situated

in the 37 positions I will use that will unleash our love
into the homeless shelters of the world
because what the fuck do they have to do tomorrow?

Every time I enter you a tine on Satan's pitchfork
bends itself over the belly of a fresh atheist.
There is room enough in our religion of nakedness
and backs to accommodate even the Philistines of Limbo,
who even now are wondering, "Whose the black guy?"

Everyone compares you to angels.
I don't want no fucking angel.
I want you to love me like wings would be in the way
blocking my view of the valley as I score you from behind
a carpenter of flesh planing the small of your back
until you can stick a needle in it and shit music.
I don't need a halo shining in the corner like a nightlight
I want to feel my way to you, where it is dark
banging my foot on your bones and cursing
until even the angels,
who have never had a good fuck in their eternal life,
wonder what the hell is going on down there?

If you know you're going to Hell, turn to page 26.
If your cousin no longer takes your calls, turn to page 105.

THE CONFESSION

To whom it may concern:
I am now a very old man
and this is something which happened to me
when I was very young – only nine years old.
It's a great relief to write this down.
This is what happened.

Once upon a time, not so long ago,
a monster came to the small town of Castle Rock, Maine.
The terror, which would not end
for another twenty-eight years – if it ever did end –
began, so far as I know or can tell,
with a boat made from a sheet of newspaper
floating down a gutter swollen with rain.

He looked like the total all-American kid
as he pedaled his twenty-six inch Schwinnn
with the apehanger handlebars up
the residential suburban street, and that's just what he was:
Todd Bowden, thirteen years old,
five-feet-eight and a healthy one hundred and forty pounds,
hair the color of ripe corn, blue eyes,
white even teeth, lightly tanned skin marred
by not even the first shadow of adolescent acne.

September 15th was his birthday,
and he got exactly what he wanted: a Sun.
Todd's mother went to the door, hesitated there,
came back, and tousled his hair.
The old man sat in the barn doorway
in the smell of apples, rocking,
wanting not to want to smoke
not because of the doctor but because now
his heart fluttered all the time.

The barbecue was over.
The guy's name was Snodgrass
and I could see him getting ready to do something crazy.
In previous years, he had always taken pride in his lawn.
I came to you because I want to tell my story,
the man on my couch was saying.
The question is: Can he do it?
The most important things are the hardest things to say.

"I've never told anyone this story,
and never thought I would – not because I was afraid
of being disbelieved, exactly, but because I was ashamed
...and because it was mine. People's lives – their real lives,
as opposed to their simple physical existences – begin at different times.
I've got a good job now, and no reason to feel glum.
But Viet Nam was over and the country was getting on.

My friend L.T. hardly ever talks about how
his wife disappeared, or how she's probably dead,
just another victim of the Axe Man, but he likes
to tell the story of how she walked out on him.
Miss Sidley was her name, and teaching was her game.
I waited and watched for seven years.
She was squinting at the thermometer
in the white light coming through the window.
Looking into the display case was like
looking through a dirty pane of glass
into the middle third of his boyhood, those years
from seven to fourteen when he had been fascinated
by stuff like this. "I know what you need."

The morning I got it on was nice; a nice May morning.
"Oh you cheap son of a bitch!" she cried
in the empty hotel room, more in surprise than in anger.
By the time the woman had gone, it was nearly
two-thirty in the morning. They had been predicting
a norther all week and along about Thursday we got it,
a real screamer that piled up eight inches
by four in the afternoon and showed no signs of slowing down.
I only saw the sign because I had to pull over and puke.

My old blue Ford pulled into the guarded parking lot
that morning, looking like a small, tired dog after a hard run.
My wife had been waiting for me since two,
and when she saw the car pull up in front of our apartment building,
she came out to meet me. I turned the radio on too loud
and didn't turn it down because we were on the verge
of another argument and I didn't want it to happen.
But sometimes the sounds – like the pain – faded,
and then there was only the haze. I tried to scream
but shock robbed my voice and I was able to produce
only a low, choked whuffing – the sound of a man moaning in his sleep.
When Mary woke up, we were lost. Considering it was
probably the end of the world, I thought she was doing a good job.
The one thing nobody asked in casual conversation,
she thought in the days after she found what she found in the garage,
was this: How's your marriage?

Officer Hunton got to the laundry just as the ambulance was leaving –
slowly, with no siren or flashing lights.
L.T.'s boy came around the barracks a lot the year after his father died,
I mean a lot, but nobody ever told him to get out the way
or asked him what in hail he was doing there again."

"Go on," Snodgrass said again. *"Look in the bag."*

It's so dark that for awhile – just how long I don't know –
I think I'm still unconscious.
It was a deathroom.

The dawn washed slowly down Culver Street.
It was forty miles from Horlicks University
in Pittsburg to Cascade Lake, and although dark comes early
to this part of the world in October
and although they didn't get going until six o'clock,
there was still a little light in the sky when they got there.
Walking to school you ask me
what other schools have grades.
It became our motto, and we couldn't for the life of us
remember which of us started saying it first.

I can't go out no more.
You've been here before.
New England autumn and the thin soil
now shows patches through the ragweed
and goldenrod, waiting for snow
still four weeks distant.

If you take the hotel job, turn to page 65.
If sometimes dead is better, turn to page 27.

TO THE QUESTION, "IF YOU HAVE SO MANY POETRY ACCOLADES, WHY ARE YOU STILL A LIBARIAN (*SIC*)?"

I'm still a librarian because, apparently,
one can get into college without knowing
how to say the word "librarian."

I'm still a librarian because instead of buying my book,
you checked it out of a library.

I'm still a librarian because a quote in the *New York Times*
isn't a paycheck from the *New York Times*.

I'm still a librarian because even the worst librarian
gets paid more than the best poet.

Poets don't have break rooms or water coolers or reserved parking.
I'm still a librarian because I enjoy owning things.
Those Playstation games aren't going to buy themselves.

I'm still a librarian because I need to be told when to stop writing.

I'm still a librarian because Kay Ryan is still a teacher.

I'm still a librarian because you don't know who Kay Ryan is.

I'm still a librarian because paychecks have a certain
je ne sais quoi about them.

I'm still a librarian because I intend to die young,
but I still want to do so in a hospital.

I'm still a librarian because you couldn't handle
my unbridled writing fury. Librarian be safety measure.

I'm still a librarian because you still think your
favorite poet got there because of their poetry.

I'm still a librarian because that is somehow
less than poet, yet more than paying bills.

I'm still a librarian because it saves more lives than poetry.

I'm still a librarian because, despite what the
Department of Labor says, "poet" is a covenant,
because "poet" is seventeen syllables
is eulogy
is back of receipt
is bottom of purse
is one-poem punk
is failed rapper
is easy way in
is most non-essential necessary thing,
while librarian is number 25-4021,
is 53k annual mean wage
is 990 jobs in my town alone
is how you sold ten books in Ohio last year.

I'm still a librarian because I still haven't written
what they need, only what they want.

I'm still a librarian because even when I wrote
what they needed, they didn't hear me
because you
were so loud.

If you pay your fine, turn to page 70.
If you keep the book just one more day, turn to page 5.

Notes

"The Janitor of *High School Musical* Speaks" appeared in
Crab Orchard Review.

"Having Dinner with Sara Littlecrow-Russell" and "Denny's Diner and
Coliseum" appeared in *Union Station Magazine*.

"To The Mother of My Enemy", "Urban Legends" and "The Confession"
appeared in *Radius*.

"Black House Party, circa 1979" appeared in *614 Magazine*.

"Sidekicks" appeared in *Multiverse* (Write Bloody Publishing).

"My Ex By Way of Review" appeared in *Pouch*.

"Rules for Playing *Stand Your Ground*" was an ekphrastic work based on
the sculpture "Pieces to Pieces" by Stephen Canneto, commissioned by the
Ohio Arts Council for the 2013 *You Call That Art?* exhibit.

"The Livingston Avenue Suite" was previously published in drastically
different form as a chapbook by Rewriting Ovid Press.

The "Clarksdale" section was previously published in slightly different
form as a chapbook, entitled *Watering Hole: Juke Joint Poems* by
Rewriting Ovid Press, and was originally composed as an ekphrastic project
based on the photography of Birney Imes.

The "Muse Arcade" section was previously released in slightly different
form as part of the *Muse Arcade* project.

Photo credit from "The Lie" is the author. Photo content is from the back
of a refurbished sharecropping shack in Clarksdale, Mississippi, located

at former plantation-now-tourist hotel, the Shack Up Inn. The rental was a very agreeable $75 a night and all the cognitive dissonance you could stand.

"To the Question, 'If You Have So Many Poetry Accolades Why Are you Still a Libarian?' (sic)" was written after a street battle that did not end well for the person who posed the question.

"The Confession" is a cento composed entirely of the first lines of Stephen King short stories and novels.

"These Aren't the Thugs You're Looking For" and "Neil deGrasse Tyson's Love Note, Third Grade" both appeared in *FreezeRay Poetry*.

Index

30797714R00071

Made in the USA
Columbia, SC
30 October 2018